INSTANT
COMMUNICATION SKILLS

Instant Communication Skills

The INSTANT-Series *Presents*

INSTANT

COMMUNICATION SKILLS

How to Improve Communications Skills Instantly!

Instant Series Publication

Copyright © Instant Series Publication

All rights reserved.

It is impermissible to reproduce any part of this book without prior consent. All violations will be prosecuted to the fullest extent of the law.

While attempts have been made to verify the information contained within this publication, neither the author nor the publisher assumes any responsibility for errors, omissions, interpretation or usage of the subject matter herein.

This publication contains the opinions and ideas of its author and is intended for informational purpose only. The author and publisher shall in no event held liable for any loss or other damages incurred from the usage of this publication.

ISBN 978-1-508-86347-2

Printed in the United States of America

First Edition

FIRST STEP:

Before proceeding, visit http://www.instantseries.com, and join the **INSTANT Newsletter** now.

You will want to! :)

Instant Communication Skills

CONTENTS

Chapter 1 - The Importance of Communication

11 - Don't Be Unheard Or Misunderstood

12 - What Is Communication?

14 - Mastering Your Communication

Chapter 2 - What to Do to Be a Better Communicator NOW

16 - Easiest And Quickest Way To Improve Communication

19 - Evaluate Before You Communicate

22 - Think-On-Your-Feet Communication

23 - Exercise: Instant Response Team

24 - Better With People, Better With Communication

24 - Exercise: Be A Silent Observer

26 - Buy Time Or Change Course With Deflection

29 - Better Communication—Best Practices

Chapter 3 - Written Communication

33 - Audio Removal

34 - Are You Bad At Written Communication?

35 - TRY IT: Hit Up A Friend

Chapter 4 - Communication Field Work

37 - Communications Boot Camp

37 - First Exercise: Analyze Difficult Phrasing

39 - Second Exercise: Giving Directions

40 - Third Exercise: Checking Perceptions

41 - Fourth Exercise: Telephone Exchange

41 - The Four Listening Tips

Chapter 5 - Communication in Action

43 - Apply Your Newfound Knowledge

43 - Use Directions

44 - Listen Up

Chapter 6 - 3 C's—Communication in Conversation for Connection

46 - The Ultimate Goal Of Communication

47 - Inspire And Invite

48 - Share Interests
49 - Involve Open-ended Questions
51 - Self-Advertising
51 - Make It A Habit

Chapter 7 - You Are NOW Equipped to Be a Better Communicator
53 - Good Communication Is Everything
54 - Go Communicate With The World

Instant Communication Skills

Chapter 1
The Importance of Communication

Don't Be Unheard Or Misunderstood

We've all been in this situation at one point or another. *You know*, the one where you crack a joke and someone else thinks you're completely serious, or majorly misinterprets what you said...

Then follows a long, awkward conversation, beginning with an embarrassed apology and ending with you falling all over yourself trying to explain what you *really* meant. Yikes!

It's moments like these that can signal a death blow to your self-esteem and make you cringe every time you think about them...or at least until you conveniently forget about them.

But if you're trying to break the ice in an awkward situation—one where you're not really in tune with the other person's personality and you're throwing out feelers with a joke or some small talk—positions like this are pretty much unavoidable.

So how come *some* people never seem to experience these embarrassing situations?

It's simple. They're in tune with the **art of proper communication**.

What Is Communication?

In this day and age, everything is centered around instant communication. Advertisements urging you to buy a specific product; one-click shopping; your cell phone giving you the ability to communicate with anyone who's ever given you their number; people around the world being able to reach you via Twitter, Facebook, and the Internet in general...

In fact, it's almost impossible *not* to have to communicate with people!

If you think about it, it seems easy to define "**communication.**" It's merely transferring and receiving the ideas of others. Simple, right?

But the hard part is communicating *effectively*.

Communication is a multifaceted process, broken down into four essential categories. The first two could be categorized as *delivery*—how you issue your communication. **Verbal** *(one's words and tone)*, **nonverbal** *(body language)*, **listening,** and last but not least, **written messages**.

Each of these can be broken down even further, but to keep it simple, let's just focus on these four concepts that make up the broader landscape of communication.

Mastering Your Communication

Learning to communicate effectively means mastering each of these *subsets* and their different *variations*. It's an ongoing learning process, one you've been practicing throughout your entire life.

One of the first and most important things you ever learned was *how* to communicate. The very basics—the ones you learned as a baby and a toddler.

In school the learning process continued, both through grammar classes and your interaction with teachers and students.

But sometimes, in order to interact with others, it's beneficial to be well versed in more complex forms of communication as well. School is (or was) merely a place where you learned those basics...or perhaps you didn't because you didn't socialize much or were homeschooled.

But now that you've gone through school, (or most of it) you may be wondering: *how much more can there be to learn about communicating?*

You've pretty much gotten the basics down, now all you have to do is **learn and master the finer details.**

No patronizing, time-wasting basics here, just fast-action ways to fine-tune your communication as well as your reception of other people's messages.

Chapter 2
What to Do to Be a Better Communicator NOW

Easiest And Quickest Way To Improve Communication

The easiest and quickest way to improve your communication skills is to work on your **body language** first.

You should become familiar with the meanings of **gestures** and **postures**—both your own and those of other people. Don't worry, this goes way beyond the cliché, *"Arms crossed means you're blocking someone out,"* spiel.

Becoming more familiar with body language means having a conscious thought about yourself and others. It's basically about being fully aware of the person you're communicating with and learning to pick up on his non-verbal clues.

This is almost an in-born skill. You already subconsciously know quite a bit about the meanings of different poses and gestures, but now you've got to learn…to bring this knowledge to the front of your mind and automatically utilize it in your everyday interactions.

You have to be able to integrate this skill as a natural part of your conversation. You don't want to be ignoring everything they're saying in order to concentrate on what they're doing, but you also don't want to miss the little twitching of the foot that means they're thoroughly fed up with the current conversation and would like to move along.

It would also completely defeat the purpose for you to not be listening to a conversation at all because you're so intent on using the right body language that you can't figure out what face to make in response to a statement that passed you by five minutes ago.

This <u>scenario</u> brings up another issue - **being aware** of body language but not *understanding* it.

Think of it like listening to a conversation in a foreign country; it's obvious that someone is trying to communicate with you, but you have no idea whether they're buying you lunch or calling the cops.

The solution to this is as simple as you think—practice and become familiar with the differences in body language, both *subtle* and *obvious*.

Think about your own reactions in different scenarios. Do you tend to lose all facial expressions if you're uncomfortable with the subject matter? Do your eyes tend to wander if you're trying to get up the courage to issue some bad news?

Be **perceptive** and attempt to *learn the meanings* of those actions you're not already familiar with.

Evaluate Before You Communicate

Another method for improving your communication skills stems from an old adage you probably heard a million times when you were a kid—*think before you speak*.

Back then, your parents telling you to *"know what you're going to say before you say it"* was to prevent you from thoughtlessly blurting out something rude.

Now you're going to reuse that concept in order to evaluate exactly what it is that you'll be communicating.

- Is what you are going to say easy to understand?

- Is it in the correct context?

- What tone of voice will you be using, and how will the other person interpret it?

Make the meaning of what you say, *and do,* as clear as possible.

This may seem time-consuming—pulling a conversation to a halt in order to think it out first—but it can really be a time saver in the long run. In other words, you won't have to waste time explaining yourself if you just get it right the first time.

By evaluating your words during a discussion, you're making sure things are as clear as possible as well as honing your ability to state your point concisely in order to avoid confusion.

Generally, people only think to evaluate their vocabulary and phrasing when the communication is written. For example, you're talking with a friend on Facebook, but before you post your comment, you look it over and eventually decide to tweak a few parts and take out that comment about their mother...

The reason this doesn't normally happen with **spoken language** is that we tend to be spouting out whatever we want to say without taking the time to think of exactly *how* we need to say it.

*Talk about a clash of the **creative mind** and the **logical mind**!* One wants to talk and the other wants to edit!

In other words, because our thoughts are being directly translated into words and immediately spoken, we normally have a hard time concentrating on the actual words themselves and making sure they're tactful and match up to the original thought.

The point is to insert this second step into the language process, allowing your words to catch up with your thoughts for better, clearer communication.

Think-On-Your-Feet Communication

Now, of course, there *are* times when you just don't have that luxury of preplanning your thoughts and evaluating what you're going to say beforehand.

There are always going to be situations where you have to be spontaneous and engage in **think-on-your-feet communication**—like on the job, at a corporate meeting, or any other fast-paced situation in which you don't have time to stop and carefully think out a response.

This is another almost instinctive skill, one that's largely governed by the right side of your brain—the side that also controls creativity and imagination. The point is, the skill is *already there*, yet does come more easily to natural creative folks.

On the other hand, if you're more logically prone, you just have to stimulate and train it more.

Exercise: Instant Response Team

Get together with a friend, and have them come up with several completely random and off-topic questions. Take them one at a time and give yourself 30 seconds to come up with a response, then have your friend grade you on the following aspects:

- Was each response logical and clearly stated?

- Did it answer the question completely?

- Did it take you the whole 30 seconds—or longer—to formulate your response?

If you made a failing grade on any of these, ask them to give you a new question, and practice until you can give an appropriate, satisfactory response in under 30 seconds.

This will be an invaluable skill to have next time you're randomly called on in a meeting by your boss. You won't embarrass yourself by stuttering and stumbling, and you'll be able to impress him with your composure and your capability. Promotion here you come!

Better With People, Better With Communication

And again, as was mentioned at the very beginning, miscommunication and awkward situations generally occur when you don't know the other party very well.

This is generally more of a problem in **social situations**, though, because chances are you won't be making personal talk in a corporate meeting.

But even in completely social situations, you still have to think on your feet in order to avoid getting floored by an unexpected question coming at you out of nowhere.

Exercise: Be A Silent Observer

This exercise goes back to the previous discussion on body language. Only with this technique, you're focusing on learning to quickly "read" and "feel out" a person, based on observation, body language, and attitude.

At the next party or gathering you attend (you can even do it in a crowded mall or a movie theater), find a conversation going on between two people comparatively unknown to you and just unobtrusively "people-watch." (Don't worry, you're not snooping, you're *researching*.)

- Pick one or the other of the party and focus on him/her (hereafter to be known as the "study").

- Give yourself 4-5 minutes to observe them. Focus on their body language, tone, and expressions and try to compose a "profile."

- When your time's up, wait until your "study" receives a question, and try to make a guess at what his/her response will be—you have just until they actually make a response.

- Since you really can't be expected to know the answers to these questions, just grade yourself on the tones and expressions that accompany the "study's" response.

- How successful were you at "predicting" reactions from your "study"?

This exercise is useful in helping you learn to compose an "instant impression" on your conversation partner in as short a time as possible. You're not trying to learn so much about his life as about his personality and disposition, so you can have a better chance of being prepared for his questions when they come.

Buy Time Or Change Course With Deflection

And lastly, another useful technique in this type of situation is **deflection.** In other words, you need to learn to be able to subtly deflect a tough question for a few minutes, in order to give yourself a little more time to prepare your answer.

If you've ever watched politicians take questions, you're probably already familiar with this maneuver. In fact, it seems to be one of the main courses they're required to take in political school. So you're going to study the experts to see how they do it.

- Find any debate video and listen to the politicians take questions—either from reporters or from each other.

- Wait until you hear this technique being used—it will be easy to spot—then rerun that section a few times and study it closely.

- Was it successful in either completely changing the trend of the conversation or at least giving the politician a few minutes of preparation time? If so, what did he/she say or do in order to deflect the question?

- Think back to a situation you were once in, one where you were asked an awkward or difficult question and you stuttered and stumbled for a while before hitting on a fairly unsatisfactory response. Now, what could you have said in order to deflect the question for a few minutes?

If you practice this technique and get it down by heart, next time you're at a party or an informal meeting and you get asked the inevitable, awkward question about your ex boy/girlfriend by a comparative stranger (hey, *everyone's* a comparative stranger in that situation), you'll be able to deflect the question by either redirecting the conversation or giving a response that doesn't commit you to anything definite.

Stopping to take a minute to think is an invaluable asset, but in cases where you have to think fast on your feet, these techniques are invaluable to maintaining communications.

Better Communication—Best Practices

Now that we have gone over dealing with the more difficult "think-on-your-feet communication," here are some additional simple tips you can put into practice for improving your overall communication.

- Engagement Enforcement—*AKA* Open-ended Questions

The first tip is to make a point—in every meaningful conversation—of coming up with a couple of provocative, relevant questions to ask the other person. This not only makes you think and concentrate harder on what is being said but also makes it easier for both parties to be thoroughly engaged in the discussion.

- Create Expected Communication Habits

Another simple thing you can do is to create a schedule around which you'll respond to emails, texts, voice mail, and so on. It's frustrating to wait for someone to respond to your own messages when you have no idea when or if they'll ever get back to you...so help the other person out when they're in your shoes.

For example, make it a point to respond to texts within twenty minutes, emails within an hour, and phone calls within a day. By following a schedule and making others around you aware of your communication habits, it will make it easier for them to be patient while anticipating your response.

Of course, you can't *always* guarantee when you can respond, but you *can* follow through on a promise. For example, if you tell someone you'll get them an answer by the end of the day, make sure you touch base then, even if you don't have their answer ready. Let them know you're still working on it and you'll follow up again tomorrow.

- **Always Filter Communication with Positivity**

Strange as it may seem, it's common to hear people complaining about the tone used in a completely innocuous email or note. This is because people tend to misinterpret the *intent* behind nonverbal communication.

For instance, if a slight animosity exists between two parties, written communication tends to escalate it. *Fast.* And this is because each person is going to read that animosity and tone into any written message they receive from the other party, whether the intent is actually there or not.

With any nonverbal communication, always start out with the assumption that the intentions behind it are good. But if you ever have any doubt…call the person up and at least give them a chance to insult you directly, if they're going to at all. That way you can at least be *sure* that you read the intent correctly.

- Be a Good Recipient

The final tip is to make sure both you and the other party know when a conversation is over and done with.

If someone texts you a message and you don't respond, they have no idea whether or not you've even read it yet. Eventually they'll start to send follow-up texts—which can be both annoying and time-consuming for all concerned.

To avoid this problem, all you have to do is acknowledge the message with a simple "*Got it*," or "*Will do*."

You may have noticed that the last few tips listed here mostly had to do with *written communication*. This is because writing has many more inherent pitfalls (which we'll get into next) than verbal communication.

Chapter 3
Written Communication

Audio Removal

What communication skills are complete without including the written aspect?

Written communication is a combination of *listening* and *speaking*…with the removal of the audible element, of course.

How does that work out? It's simple. You still have the language, words, phrasing, and tone (or *nonverbal tone* shall we say)—they're just applied and received in a different manner.

Since this is so, any of the tips for speaking and listening can apply to written messages as well—the techniques for clear and concise communication, for example.

And that brings us on to the next topic, which is...recognizing bad writing habits.

Are You Bad At Written Communication?

As you read the following statements, think about how closely they each apply to you and which of the previously mentioned techniques you can use to improve them.

- I don't read the other person's message thoroughly and often miss important details.

- I don't give any response to a message, even if I say I will.

- I tend to ramble and go on too long.

- I tend to misinterpret tone when I'm angry.

- I am not good at clearly phrasing ideas or questions.

- I have a hard time getting words on paper.

For the majority of these problems, just remember: the **core of written communication** is simply speaking and listening *without audio*.

In other words, the intent is there and the message is there, even the tone is there (but that's an interpretation left almost entirely to the reader)—all you have to do is put words to paper just as you'd speak them aloud.

So try applying some of the previous methods to your written—as well as verbal-communications.

<u>TRY IT</u>: Hit Up A Friend

Now that you have a good idea of how improve your communications (nonverbal, verbal, and written), take some time to **try out** the knowledge you've acquired.

Step away now and get in touch with a friend to practice these communication techniques in person. If you can't manage a face-to-face chat, pick a fairly complicated message and shoot it across to them. Email, text—it doesn't matter.

- Did you manage to get your message across on the first try?

- If you were sending written messages, did you chase rings around each other trying to nail down the idea, or did you manage to successfully organize your response system?

Once you've evaluated your result, either return and proceed for more in-depth exercises or keep at it until you can get a message right on the first try.

Chapter 4
Communication Field Work

Communications Boot Camp

Now that you're familiar with the methods and techniques you'll be using, it's time for some serious **Communications Boot Camp** to start practicing and see improvement.

You know you're excited!

Work hard here, and you'll be able to play harder with the results.

First Exercise: Analyze Difficult Phrasing

Get out your college copy of *Hamlet* or Dante's *Inferno* (or any other intricate reading material) and look for absolutely anything that doesn't make sense.

Concentrate on the different quotes and passages. Think about them, analyze them, and do your best to comprehend the meaning—only using the Internet if absolutely necessary. Yes, this is ancient stuff and the words are archaic at best, but that's not the point. The point is that you're sharpening your "deciphering" skills and learning to **interpret** more accurately.

- How long did it take you to get through some of the more difficult pages?

- When you've finished a few passages, Google them and see how close your interpretations are to the ones shown there.

- If the explanations differ quite a bit from how you understood them, go back to the book and, armed with the notes, see if the passages make more sense this time.

Second Exercise: Giving Directions

Everyone knows about the whole *"wives and directions"* bit. But in all honesty, guys are just as bad as girls.

If you've ever ended up in the Sahara because he said *left* at the stop sign instead of *right*, then you can relate to the emotions here.

But the whole problem is that, usually, giving directions to someone means that they initially have no idea what you're talking about.

They're unfamiliar with the environment you're describing, and they're relying on you to describe it accurately enough that they can understand where they're going and where they've been.

Give directions or instructions for somebody to follow; can be as random as picking up a very specific type of detergent or Grade A eggs. Even better, teach someone some complicated concepts.

That said, the main purpose of this exercise is to work on your ability to simplify and convey unfamiliar messages to someone else.

Third Exercise: Checking Perceptions

Get one of your friends on the phone and either tell them a story or have them tell you one.

- Once they've finished, repeat what you heard…or listen to what the other person thinks you said.

- Communicating as concisely and clearly as possible, find out where any misunderstandings came in and explain the real concept.

<u>Fourth Exercise</u>: Telephone Exchange

Remember that old game "Telephone" you and your friends played in elementary school? You'd whisper something in the next person's ear, then they'd pass it on to the next person, and so on until it had gone full circle. Then the last person would tell you what the final version of the message was.

This is another excellent communication exercise for both yourself and others—as long as none of you decide it would be funny to garble the message on purpose. *That sort of defeats the whole point of the exercise!*

- Did the message stay essentially the same?

- If not, find out where the message was garbled and try again.

The Four Listening Tips

These next tips really aren't so much exercises as they are advice to live by…so take them to heart and use them during every meaningful conversation:

1. Paraphrase the speaker's message back to him in order to confirm your understanding. Put the message in your own words. This way you have to concentrate harder on the actual *meaning* of what's being said, rather than just the wording.

2. Probe for missing information. By asking questions or requesting them from the audience, you can pinpoint any pertinent information that may have been missing.

3. Clarify any points you don't completely understand. The explanation for this one is fairly self-evident.

4. Don't try to remember each and every syllable of the message. It's a waste of time and "head-space." Instead, just define the main points and catalogue them for future reference.

Chapter 5
Communication in Action

Apply Your Newfound Knowledge

Now that you've gone through and, hopefully, done all the communication exercises *(If not, go back and do them now. This knowledge is useless without practice!)...*

It's time to put to use what you've learned about communicating clearly and understanding fully. You are now going to apply this knowledge to real world situations.

Use Directions

For example, giving directions such as in the **Second Exercise**...

The example in that exercise was for a specific situation, but there are many, many other scenarios in which you can use the techniques outlined in the exercise. For instance, describing the model of the car you own to an inexperienced auto-shop employee while searching for replacement parts...

Or trying to describe that certain dress or pair of tennis shoes you want your spouse to pick up when he/she goes shopping.

Listen Up

As for the **Four Listening Tips,** make a point of using them to properly comprehend and remember what someone else is saying when they're on the speaking end of the conversation. Make sure you have and understand all the information and that you're remembering only the important details.

Use these tips to remember that item your significant other wants. For example:

1. The dress was at Macy's.
2. It was on a mannequin.
3. It was red, white, and knee-length.
4. She needs a size 6.

You've made sure you have all the necessary info—you're not going to accidentally bring her a size 12—but you're not wasting time with the unimportant details.

Chapter 6
3 C's—Communication in Conversation for Connection

The Ultimate Goal Of Communication

What is the first thing that comes to mind when you hear the word "communication"?

It's probably two people speaking and holding a **conversation**, *right?*

That's because one of the more popular purposes of conversation is to *use communication to form a connection* or *build rapport* with another person.

The following are various tips and techniques to use when engaging in conversation:

Inspire And Invite

There are two important factors to holding a meaningful conversation—**inspiration** and **invitation**.

Inspire the other party to share their thoughts, curiosity, and/or their story.

For example, if you're talking about your trip to the beach, ask them about their last vacation, or phrase your information in a way that opens a path for them to comment, expressing their thoughts and/or curiosity about your trip.

A good, basic technique to initiate this without asking the other person directly…is to share your thoughts on the topic at hand. The other person will feel inclined to add their opinions or questions, in order to redirect attention back to themselves, then eventually you'll do the same again, either to keep up the flow of their thoughts or to seek new information.

This is how the **back-and-forth motion** of a conversation is created.

A conversation is based entirely on **attention** and **information**. Without catering to one or the other of those two concepts, an active discussion cannot take place.

Share Interests

Another great way to implement this technique is to use your knowledge of the other party's interests in order to introduce a similar subject that you know will capture their attention.

For example, if you know the other person enjoys watching *Let's Players* on YouTube, bring up the fact that you love watching *PewDiePie* or *Game Grumps*.

This paves the way for you both to discuss similar interests, building rapport and initiating further conversation such as, *"What's your favorite episode?"* or, *"Remember when Arin said...?"*

If you know of interests you share with the other person, there's no quicker way to start up a conversation than to bring those interests into the spotlight.

Involve Open-ended Questions

We've discussed these open-ended questions once already, but there's no way to over-emphasize their importance to a conversation.

They especially come in handy when you don't know the other party very well.

For example, instead of asking, *"How was your weekend?"* which would most likely result in a simple, *"Fine,"* or, *"Great, thanks,"* try asking them *what they did* this weekend.

This evokes a longer, more detailed response, giving you more content to comment on and to compare to your own experiences, thus keeping the conversation supplied with interesting material.

Inviting the other person to continue a conversation in this manner clearly shows them that it's their turn to talk, and gives them a ready-made talking point... making it simple for them to carry on the discussion.

Start out with more **superficial questions,** such as the example above, and gradually move on toward more **important topics**.

But keep in mind that this transition may not happen over the course of one conversation. Give it some time and, eventually, discussion will flow more smoothly and naturally.

Self-Advertising

Another part of the invitation factor of conversation is **self-advertising**.

Let others sell themselves to you. It may be a bit boring, but giving the other party first go will make them feel as if you really value what they have to say. So listen *patiently*—no foot-tapping, fidgeting, or glancing at your watch.

Once they've finished, find out where they're going with this conversation and what you can do for them.

By having them clarify what they expect of you, you can both live up to *their* expectations and more easily convince them to meet your own.

Make It A Habit

By combining these techniques for initiating conversation with the techniques for clarity and conciseness, you should be able to start a conversation anywhere and anytime with perfect success.

But of course, it's obvious that you're not going to become a professional communicator overnight—like anything else, you have to *practice* these exercises constantly in real, face-to-face (or email-to-email) conversations before you can truly see improvement.

Chapter 7
You Are NOW Equipped to Be a Better Communicator

Good Communication Is Everything

Excellent communication comes with many benefits—decreased frustration and misgivings over whether or not you were clearly understood, assuring both you and the other party that you understood what *they* were talking about, being able to smoothly avoid or pass over awkward situations, etc.

Communication is the foundation of our society and life would be next to impossible without it. Speaking, listening, writing, and body language have been uniting—and separating—people for thousands of years. But no matter which of the four main concepts you struggle with, there *are* methods for improving.

By making yourself aware of your own faults in the communication department and by working to improve them, you'll make life infinitely easier for both yourself and those around you.

Go Communicate With The World

Having gone through your entire communication training...

You have consciously learned about your communication skills, those of people around you, and how communication works in our society as a whole.

Congratulations on taking this step toward the clearer, less complicated life that comes from the power of effective communication skills!

Instant Communication Skills

55 - INSTANT Series

An INSTANT Thank You!

Thank you for entrusting in the <u>INSTANT Series</u> to help you improve your life.

Our goal is simple, help you achieve instant results as fast as possible in the quickest amount of time. We hope we have done our job, and you have gotten a ton of value.

If you are in any way, shape, or form, dissatisfied, then please we encourage you to get refunded for your purchase because we only want our readers to be happy.

If, *on the other hand*, you've enjoyed it, if you can kindly leave us a review on where you have purchased this book, that would mean a lot.

What is there to do now?

Simple! Head over to http://www.instantseries.com, and sign up for our **newsletter** to stay up-to-date with the latest instant developments *(if you haven't done so already)*.

Be sure to check other books in the INSTANT Series. If there is something you like to be added, be sure to let us know for as always we love your feedback.

Yes, we're on **social medias**. *Don't forget to follow us!*

https://www.facebook.com/InstantSeries

https://twitter.com/InstantSeries

https://plus.google.com/+Instantseries

Thank you, and wish you all the best!
- *The INSTANT Series Team*

Instant Communication Skills

59 - INSTANT Series

Printed in Great Britain
by Amazon